A Music Enthusiast's Guide to

Songs You Should
Have on Your I-Pod

Without music life would be a mistake.

Friedrich Nietzsche

Music is to the mind as air to the body. Plato

Without music, life is a journey through a desert.

Pat Conroy

I think popular music in this country is one of the few things in the 20th century that have made great strides in reverse. Bing Crosby

A Music Enthusiast's Guide to

Songs You Should Have on Your I-Pod

Over 2000 Songs From Over 500 Bands

♫♪ ♫♪ ♪ ♫♪♫

Compiled and Edited by:

J. R. McManus

iUniverse, Inc.
New York   Bloomington

A Music Enthusiast's Guide to
Songs You Should Have on Your I-Pod

iUniverse books may be ordered through booksellers or by contacting:

iUniverse
1663 Liberty Drive
Bloomington, IN 47403
www.iuniverse.com
1-800-Authors (1-800-288-4677)

ISBN: 978-1-4401-5343-3 (sc)
ISBN: 978-1-4401-5344-0 (ebk)

Printed in the United States of America

iUniverse rev. date: 09/01/2009

Dedicated to my dad who first introduced me to good music.

Introduction

I have always been a fan of music. To me a good song is a good song regardless of when it was written. It could have been written 5 weeks ago or 50 years ago. Some songs, when done right, are simply timeless. I started off by writing a blog of songs and bands people should listen to. It was intended to introduce the young folk to bands that they may normally not listen to, like bands from the 60's, 70's, etc. From there it morphed into me compiling a list of bands and songs that I love and that never get old. Of course the list is subjective and a continual work in progress. I scoured my own, my family's and my friends' record collections to create a list of bands, musicians and songs that are simply good. Some were popular while others were more obscure. Some songs were number one hits while others were rare tracks, deeper cuts and B-sides. I have also included one hit wonders and songs that I like to call Guilty Pleasures. Songs and bands you may never admit you like or listen to but somehow you know all of the words and sing along to them when they come on the radio as long as no one else is around. Regardless of their commercial and chart success these are **Songs You Should Have on Your I-Pod.**

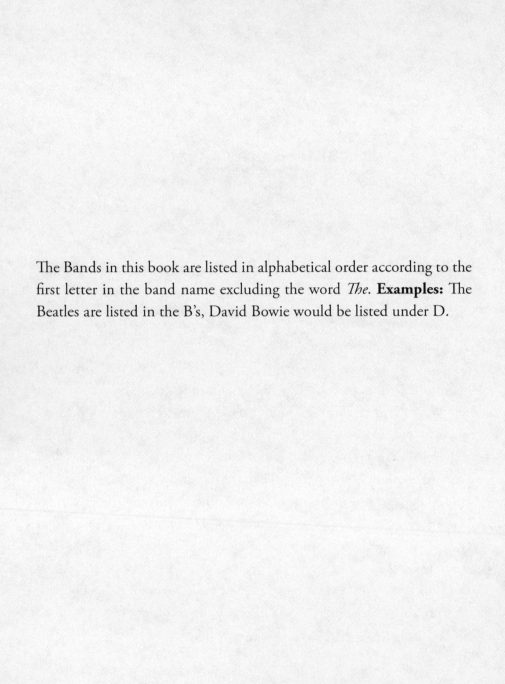

The Bands in this book are listed in alphabetical order according to the first letter in the band name excluding the word *The*. **Examples:** The Beatles are listed in the B's, David Bowie would be listed under D.

A

AC/DC:
Ain't No Fun (waiting around to
    be a millionaire)
Back in Black
Big Balls
Dirty Deeds Done Dirt Cheap
For Those About To Rock
    (We Salute You)
Have a Drink On Me
Hells Bells
High Voltage
Highway to Hell
It's a Long Way to the Top
    (If You Wanna Rock N' Roll)
Let There Be Rock
Live Wire
Moneytalks
Problem Child
Rock N' Roll Train
Shoot to Thrill
Shot Down in Flames
Squealer
Stiff Upper Lip
Thunderstruck
T.N.T
Whole Lotta Rosie
You Shook Me All Night Long

The Adverts:
Gary Gilmore's Eye's
No Time to be 21

Aerosmith:
Baby, Please Don't Go
Back in the Saddle
Come Together
Crazy
Cryin'
Dream On
Dude (Looks Like a Lady)
Falling in Love (Is Hard on the
    Knees)
I Don't Want To Miss A Thing
Jaded
Janie's Got a Gun
Livin' on the Edge
Love in an Elevator
Mama Kin
Pink
Rag Doll
Same Old Song and Dance
Sweet Emotion
Train Kept a Rollin
Walk This Way

Agent Orange:
Bloodstains

A-Ha
Take On Me

The Airborne Toxic Event:
Does This Mean You're Moving
    On
Gasoline
Happiness is Over
Innocence
Missy

The Airborne Toxic Event (Cont):
Something New
Sometime Around Midnight
This is Nowhere
Wishing Well

Alanis Morissette:
Hand in My Pocket
Head Over Heals
Ironic
You Learn
You Oughta Know

Alien Ant Farm:
Movies
Smooth Criminal

Alice Cooper:
Eighteen
No More Mr. Nice Guy
Only Women Bleed
Poison
School's Out

Alice in Chains:
Heaven Beside You
Man in the Box
Rooster

Alkaline Trio:
Calling All Skeletons
Help Me
Mercy Me
Stupid Kid
We've Had Enough

The All American Rejects:
Gives You Hell
Swing Swing

The Allman Brothers Band:
Ain't Wastin' Time No More
Black Hearted Woman
Jessica
Melissa
Midnight Rider
Blue Sky
One Way Out
Ramblin' Man
Revival
Statesboro Blues
Whipping Post

America:
All the Lonely People
Horse With No Name
Sister Golden Hair

Amy Winehouse:
Back to Black
Rehab

Andrew W.K.:
I Get Wet
Party Hard
She is Beautiful

20 Great Instrumental Songs:

1. **Allman Brothers Band:** Jessica
2. **Jeff Beck:** Amazing Grace
3. **Booker T & The MGs:** Green Onions
4. **Dick Dale:** Misirlou
5. **Led Zeppelin:** Moby Dick
6. **The Who:** Sparks
7. **The Who:** Overture
8. **Jimi Hendrix:** Star Spangled Banner
9. **Jeff Beck:** A Day in the Life
10. **Santana:** Soul Sacrifice
11. **Van Halen:** Eruption
12. **The Beatles:** Flying
13. **Edgar Winter:** Frankenstein
14. **Duane Eddy:** Rebel Rouser
15. **The Ventures:** Walk Don't Run
16. **The Chantays:** Pipeline
17. **The Sufaris:** Wipe Out
18. **Santo and Johnny:** Sleepwalk
19. **Booker T & The MGs:** Time is Tight
20. **Duane Eddy:** Peter Gunn

Angus & Julia Stone:
Hollywood
Just a Boy
Paper Aeroplane
Wasted

The Animals:
Don't Let Me Be Misunderstood
House of the Rising Sun
I Put a Spell on You
We Gotta Get Out of This Place

Antsy Pants:
Tree Hugger
Vampire

The Archies:
Sugar, Sugar

Arckid:
Conversation
I'll Stick Around
Narrow Streets

Arctic Monkeys:
Brainstorm
Love Machine

Aretha Franklin:
Chain of Fools
Freeway of Love
I Never Loved A Man
Natural Woman
Think
Respect

Argent:
God Gave Rock N Roll to You
Hold Your Head Up
Liar
Thunder & Lightning

Arlo Guthrie:
Alice's Restaurant
City of New Orleans
Coming into Los Angeles

Audioslave:
Doesn't Remind Me
Vampire

Avril Lavigne:
Complicated
Happy Ending

B

Bad Company:
Bad Company
Black Betty
Can't Get Enough
Feel Like Makin' Love
How About That
Rock and Roll Fantasy
Rock Steady
Shooting Star
Silver, Blue and Gold

Badfinger:
Baby Blue
Come and Get It
Day After Day
No Matter What

The Band:
Evangeline
The Night They Drove Old Dixie
   Down
The Weight
Up on Cripple Creek

The Bangles:
Walk Like an Egyptian

Barenaked Ladies:
Brian Wilson
It's All Been Done
One Week

Barenaked Ladies (Cont):
Pinch Me
The Old Apartment

Barrett Strong:
Money (That's What I Want)

Barry Louis Polisar:
All I Want is You

Barry McGuire:
Eve of Destruction

B.B. King:
How Blue Can You Get
Let the Good Times Roll
Sweet Sixteen
The Thrill Is Gone

The Beach Boys:
Barbara Ann
California Girls
Dance, Dance, Dance
Don't Worry Baby
Fun Fun Fun
God Only Knows
Good Vibrations
Hang Onto Your Ego
Help Me Rhonda
I Get Around
In My Room
Sloop John B
Surfin' Safari
Surfin' USA
Wouldn't it be Nice

The Beastie Boys:
Body Movin'
Brass Monkey
Fight for Your Right
Girls
Intergalactic
No Sleep 'Til Brooklyn
Sabotage
She's Crafty
So What'cha Want
Sure Shot

The Beatles:
Across The Universe
Act Naturally
A Day in the Life
A Hard Day's Night
All Together Now
All You Need is Love
And I Love Her
And Your Bird Can Sing
Another Girl
Baby You're a Rich Man
Blackbird
Can't Buy Me Love
Carry That Weight
Come Together
Day Tripper
Dear Prudence
Dizzy Miss Lizzie
Don't Let Me Down
Don't Pass Me By
Do You Want To Know A Secret?
Drive My Car
Dr. Robert
Eleanor Rigby

The Beatles (Cont):
Everybody's Got Something to
     Hide (Except Me and My
     Monkey)
Flying
For You Blue
Get Back
Getting Better
Golden Slumbers
Good Morning Good Morning
Got to Get You Into My Life
Happiness is a Warm Gun
Hello Goodbye
Help
Here Comes the Sun
Helter Skelter
Hey Bulldog
Hey Jude
Hold Me Tight
I Am the Walrus
I'll Follow the Sun
I'm a Looser
I'm Down
I'm Happy Just to Dance With You
I'm Looking Through You
In My Life
I Saw Her Standing There
I Should Have Known Better
It's All to Much
It Won't be Long
I've Got a Feeling
I've Just Seen a Face
I Want to Hold Your Hand
Lady Madonna
Let it Be
Long Tall Sally
Lovely Rita

Beatles' Songs That Don't Often Get Played on the Radio

There are a lot of people who consider The Beatles to be the greatest band of all time. Across the country there are a number of daily and weekly radio programs that play nothing but Beatles' music. Some play rare outtakes, studio sessions, live cuts, along with interviews of the Fab Four. However, there tends to be a specific set of songs that you always hear on the radio. Now, these songs are great, such as *Hey Jude, Let it Be* and *Revolution*, but here are just a few songs from their catalog that don't often get played on the radio.

Two of Us

She's a Woman

I've Just Seen a Face

I've Got a Feeling

Everybody's Got Something to Hide (Except Me and My Monkey)

Helter Skelter

Hey Bulldog

I'm Down

I'm Looking Through You

Getting Better

For You Blue

Baby You're a Rich Man

The Beatles (Cont):
Love Me Do
Lucy in the Sky with Diamonds
Maggie May
Magical Mystery Tour
Michelle
No Reply
Norwegian Wood (This Bird has Flown)
One After 909
Paperback Writer
Penny Lane
Please Mr. Postman
Please Please Me
Rain
Revolution
Rock and Roll Music
Rocky Raccoon
Roll Over Beethoven
Run For Your Life
Sgt. Pepper's Lonely Hearts Club Band
She Loves You
She Said She Said
She's a Woman
Something
Strawberry Fields Forever
Tax Man
The Ballad of John and Yoko
The Continuing Story of Bungalow Bill
Ticket to Ride
Tomorrow Never Knows
Twist and Shout
Two of Us
While My Guitar Gently Weeps

The Beatles (Cont):
With a Little Help From My Friends
Yesterday
You Can't Do That
You're Gonna Lose That Girl
You've Got to Hide Your Love Away

Beck:
Black Tambourine
Devils Haircut
E-Pro
Hollow Log
Loser
Lost Cause
Mixed Bizness
Nausea
Nobody's Fault but My Own
Orphans
Pay No Mind (Snoozer)
Sexx Laws
The New Pollution
Think I'm in Love
Tropicalia
Where it's At

Belle & Sebastian:
Expectations
Piazza, New York Catcher

Ben E. King (Drifters):
Save the Last Dance
Stand By Me
Under the Boardwalk

Paul is Dead?

So you're the most famous band of all time. What do you do to break up the monotony of touring, endless interviews, and long hours in the recording studio? How about you put hidden messages on your albums and in your songs that one of the founding members of the band is dead and has been replaced by a look alike.

Urban Legend has it that on Wednesday November 9, 1966 at 5 am while working in the studio on what would become the Sgt. Pepper album McCartney left the studio after an argument with the other Beatles. While driving down the road he picked up a woman, who was hitch hiking, named Rita. When she realized that it was Paul McCartney that had picked her up she got overly excited and caused Paul to lose control of his car and crash. In the accident he suffered a head injury (some speculate he was decapitated) and died. The remaining Beatles feared that this would ruin their success so they decided to replace McCartney with William Shears Campbell, a police officer, who had won a Paul McCartney lookalike contest a few years earlier. Allegedly the remaining Beatles felt guilty and remorseful for continuing on and so they left clues to the untimely death of Paul McCartney on their albums for the fans to decipher.

Album Clues

Sgt. Pepper

If you look closely at the ground in front of the assembled group, it looks like freshly dug earth. It is surrounded by flowers, some of which are in the shape of a bass guitar.

There is a hand over the head of Paul allegedly a sign of death in eastern religions or a priest blessing Paul.

The wax dummy Beatles all look very sad and are looking down at the "grave" obviously in mourning.

The Beatles are all holding brass instruments except for Paul. He is holding a wood instrument, his brass instrument is sitting next to Ringo's feet.

If you hold a mirror to the middle of the bass drum on the cover it says He Die with an arrow pointing up to Paul.

The inside photo of the band shows Paul with a patch on his left arm which reads "O.P.D." or, "Officially Pronounced Dead." Other sources say that it stands for "Ontario Provincial Police," where William Campbell was an officer when he won the infamous look-alike contest

Magical Mystery Tour:

The album came with a 24 page booklet that contained images from the movie.

On page 3 of the booklet, Paul is shown sitting behind a desk with a nameplate that reads "I Was".

In the picture of the band Paul is barefoot and his shoes are next to Ringo's bass drum with what looks like blood dripping from them. Then on Ringo's drum it says "Love the 3 Beatles."

On page 23, the Beatles are all wearing carnations, but Paul's is black while the other Beatles have red ones.

The White Album:

The White album came with a fold out poster that contained a collage of pictures

In the lower right hand corner of the poster is a picture of Paul dancing. When viewed closely, a pair of ghostly hands are reaching toward Paul from behind.

Abby Road:

On the cover each member is dressed as a specific person in a funeral. John is the minister, Ringo the pallbearer, Paul the corpse (he is also barefoot an alleged custom in Italy of burying people without their shoes and his eyes are closed) and George is the grave digger.

On the back of the album there are a number of dots next to where it says Beatles. If you connect the dots it will make the number 3, signifying the 3 remaining Beatles.

Song Clues:

At the end of *Strawberry Fields Forever* you hear John Lennon say "I buried Paul."

If you play the gibberish at the end of *I'm So Tired* backwards you will hear John saying "Paul is a dead man miss him, miss him."

If you play *Revolution #9* backwards it says "Turn me on dead man" repeatedly.

In the song *She's Leaving Home* there is the line "Wednesday Morning at 5 O'clock as the day begins" Pointing to the time when Paul had his accident.

In *Sgt. Pepper's Lonely Hearts Club Band* we are introduced to Billy Shears, short for Paul's replacement William Shears Campbell.

In a *Day in the Life*, the man who "blew his mind out in a car" is supposedly a reference to Paul and his head injury sustained in the accident.

In the song *Glass Onion* John sings, "Here's another clue for you all, the walrus is Paul." First, a glass onion is a casket with a glass top and the walrus is supposed to be a symbol of the dead or death in some mythologies

In *Don't Pass me By* there's the line "You were in a car crash and you lost your hair." Another reference to Paul's car accident.

Of course you can do a simple internet search and come up with hundreds of other clues that allege Paul is dead these were just a few of the most popular.

Ben Folds (Five):
Army
Battle of Who Could Care Less
Brick
Rockin' the Suburbs

Ben Harper:
Burn to Shine
Steal My Kisses

Better Than Ezra:
Desperately Wanting
Good

Big Audio Dynamite:
Rush

Big Country:
In a Big Country

Big Star:
Feel
I'm in Love With a Girl
In the Street
Mod Lang
Nightime
O My Soul
September Gurls
Thirteen
Watch the Sunrise

Bill Haley and his Comets:
Rock Around the Clock

Billy Holiday:
Strange Fruit
Summertime

Billy Idol:
Cradle of Love
Dancing With Myself
Eyes Without A Face
Hot in the City
Lemon Tree
Mony Mony
Rebel Yell
White Wedding

Billy Joel:
Allentown
A Matter of Trust
Captain Jack
Goodnight Saigon
It's Still Rock N' Roll to Me
Just the Way You Are
Keeping the Faith
Miami 2017
My Life
New York State of Mind
Only the Good Die Young
Piano Man
Pressure
River of Dreams
Scenes from an Italian Restaurant
She's Gotta Way
Stranger
Summer Highland Falls
The Ballad of Billy the Kid
The Entertainer
You May Be Right

Billy Joel (Cont):
You're My Home
We Didn't Start the Fire

Billy Squire:
Everybody Wants You
Lonely is the Night
My Kinda Lover
Rock Me Tonite
The Stroke

The Black Crowes:
Hard to Handle
Jealous Again
Oh Josephine
Remedy
She Talks to Angels
Twice as Hard

The Black Eyed Peas:
Pump It
Where is the Love

Black Rebel Motorcycle Club:
Ain't No Easy Way
Berlin
Love Burns
Shuffle Your Feet
Spread Your Love
We're All in Love
Whatever Happened to my Rock
   N' Roll

Black Sabbath:
Black Sabbath
Electric Funeral
Iron Man
Paranoid
N.I.B
Sweet Leaf
The Wizard
War Pigs

Blind Faith:
Can't Find My Way Back Home
Well Alright

Blind Melon:
No Rain

Blink 182:
Adam's Song
All the Small Things
Dammit
First Date
Stay Together for the Kids
The Rock Show
What's My Age Again?

Blondie:
Call Me
Heart of Glass
One Way or Another
Maria
Rapture
The Tide Is High

Bloodhound Gang:
Fire, Water, Burn
The Bad Touch

Blue Cheer:
Summertime Blues

Blue October:
Calling You
Hate Me
Into the Ocean

Blues Image:
Ride Captain Ride

Blue Oyster Cult:
Burnin' for You
(Don't Fear) The Reaper
Godzilla

Blues Traveler:
But Anyway
Hook
Run Around

Blur:
Song 2
You're So Great

Bobby Bland:
Stormy Monday Blues

The Bobby Fuller Four:
I Fought the Law

Bob Dylan:
A Hard Rain is A-Gonna Fall
All Along the Watch Tower
Blowin in the Wind
Bob Dylan's Dream
Desolation Row
Forever Young
Girl from the North Country
Highway 61 Revisited
Hurricane
I Shall Be Free
It Ain't Me Babe
I Want You
Just Like a Woman
Knocking on Heavens Door
Like a Rolling Stone
Lil Rosemary and the Jack of
    Hearts
Maggie's Farm
Most Likely You Go Your Way
    and I'll Go Mine
Mr. Tambourine Man
Obviously 5 Believers
Positively 4th Street
Rainy Day Women #12 & 35
Shelter from the Storm
Someday Baby
Subterranean Homesick Blues
Talkin' World War III Blues
Tangled Up in Blue
These Times They Are
    A-Changin'
Visions of Johanna

Bob Marley:
Buffalo Soldier
Could You Be Loved

Bob Marley (Cont):
Get Up, Stand Up
I Shot the Sheriff
Is This Love
Jamming
No Woman No Cry
One Love/ People Get Ready
Rastaman Chant
Redemption Song
Stir It Up
Three Little Birds

Bob Seger:
Against the Wind
Fire Down Below
Hollywood Nights
Like a Rock
Night Moves
Old Time Rock & Roll
Ramblin' Gamblin' Man
Turn the Page
You'll Accompany Me

Bo Diddley:
Bo Diddley
I'm a Man
Who Do You Love?

Bon Jovi:
Bad Medicine
Blame It on the Love of Rock &
    Roll
Everyday
I'll Be There for You
It's My Life
Keep the Faith

Bon Jovi (Cont):
Last Cigarette
Lay Your Hands on Me
Livin' on a Prayer
Runaway
Story of My Life
Wanted Dead or Alive
Who Says You Can't Go Home
You Give Love a Bad Name

Booker T and the MG's:
Boot-Leg
Green Onions
Time is Tight

Boston:
Let Me Take You Home Tonight
More Than a Feeling

Bowling for Soup:
Girl All The Bad Guys Want
High School Never Ends
1985

The Box Tops:
The Letter

The Bravery:
An Honest Mistake
Believe
Fearless
No Breaks
Time Won't Let Me Go
Unconditional

The Breeders:
Cannonball
Divine Hammer
Huffer
Saints

Brett Dennen:
Ain't No Reason

The Brian Setzer Orchestra:
Jump Jive An' Wail
Rock this Town
Sleepwalk

Bright Eyes:
Another Travelin' Song
A Perfect Sonnet
At the Bottom of Everything
Bowl of Oranges
Cleanse Song
Easy, Lucky, Free
First Day of My Life
If the Brakeman Turns My Way
If Winter Ends
Land Locked Blues
Loose Leaves
Make War
Road to Joy
Soul Singer in a Session Band
Waist of Paint

Bruce Springsteen (and the E-Street Band):
Adam Raised a Cain
Atlantic City
Bad Lands

Bruce Springsteen (Cont):
Born in the USA
Born to Run
Brilliant Disguise
Dancing in the Dark
Devils and Dust
Ghost of Tom Joad
Girls In Their Summer Clothes
Glory Days
Hungry Heart
I'm on Fire
Jersey Girl
My City of Ruins
No Surrender
Radio Nowhere
Reason to Believe
Rosalita (Come Out Tonight)
Streets of Philadelphia
Tenth Avenue Freeze Out
The Rising
The River
The Wrestler
Thunder Road

Bryan Adams:
Summer of '69

BTO:
Taking Care of Business
You Ain't Seen Nothing Yet

Buddy Holly:
Dearest
Everyday
Not Fade Away
Peggy Sue

Buddy Holly (Cont):
Rave On
That'll be the Day

Buffalo Springfield:
Broken Arrow
For What it's Worth
Mr.Soul

The Buggles:
Video Killed the Radio Star

Bukka White:
Fixin' to Die Blues

Bush:
Chemicals Between Us
Glycerin
Greedy Fly
Little Things
Machinehead
Mouth

The Butthole Surfers:
Cough Syrup
Pepper
TV Star

The Buzzcocks:
Autonomy
Ever Fallen in Love (With
    Someone You Shouldn'T've)
Oh Shit
Promises
What Do I Get

The Byrds:
Eight Miles High
Mr. Tambourine Man
Not Fade Away
So You Want To Be a Rock &
    Roll Star
Turn Turn Turn

The B-52's:
Funplex
Love Shack
Rock Lobster

C

Cage the Elephant:
Ain't No Rest for the Wicked
Back Against the Wall
In One Ear

Cake:
I Will Survive
Never There
Sheep go to Heaven
Short Skirt/Long Jacket
The Distance

Camper Van Beethoven:
Pictures of Matchstickmen
Sweethearts
Take the Skinheads Bowling
Wasted

Candlebox:
Far Behind

Canned Heat:
Going up the Country

The Cardigans:
Lovefool
My Favorite Game

Carl Perkins:
Blue Suede Shoes
Matchbox

Cars:
Drive
Good Times Roll
Just What I Needed
My Best Friends Girl
You're All I've Got Tonight

Cat Stevens:
Peace Train
Wild World

Chad & Jeremy:
A Summer Song

Chairlift:
Bruises

The Chantay's:
Pipeline
Surf Rat

Cheap Trick:
Gonna Raise Hell
I Want You to Want Me
Ready or Not
Surrender

Chemical Brothers:
Galvanize
Let Forever Be
Setting Sun
The Golden Path

Chicago:
25 or 6 to 4

Chuck Berry:
Johnny B. Goode
Maybellene
Rock & Roll Music
Roll Over Beethoven
Sweet Little 16

Circle Jerks:
Live Fast Die Young
Wild in the Streets

The Clash:
Clampdown
Complete Control
Guns of Brixton
I Fought the Law
London Calling
Rock the Casbah
Should I Stay or Should I Go
Train in Vain
White Riot

Cloud Cult:
Lucky Today
Pretty Voice

Cold Play:
Clocks
In My Place
Lost
The Scientist
Violet Hill

Cold Play (Cont):
Viva La Vida
Yellow

Collective Soul:
December
Forgiveness
Gel
Heavy
Hollywood
Listen
Precious Declaration
Run
She Said
Shine
Smashing Young Man
The World I Know
Why pt. 2

Common:
G.O.D.

Conor Oberst:
Cape Canaveral
I Don't Want To Die (In the
    Hospital)
NYC-Gone, Gone
Sausalito

Coolio:
Gangsters Paradise

The Coral:
Dreaming of You
In the Morning

The Coral (Cont):
Pass It On
Put the Sun Back

Cornershop:
Brimful of Asha

Counting Crows:
A Long December
Big Yellow Taxi
Hangin' Around
Mr. Jones
Round Here

Cracker:
Get Off This
Low

Cramps:
Bikini Girls with Machine Guns
Garbagemen
Goo Goo Muck
Love Me Falling Down the Stairs
Surfin Bird

The Cranberries:
Dreams
Linger
Zombie

Cream:
Badge
Crossroads
I Feel Free

Cream (Cont):
I'm so Free
I'm So Glad
Strange Brew
Sunshine of Your Love
SWLABR
Tales of Brave Ulysses
Toad
White Room

Credence Clearwater Revival:
Bad Moon Rising
Born on the Bayou
Down on the Corner
Fortunate Son
Grapevine (Heard It Through)
Green River
Have You Ever Seen the Rain
It Came Out of the Sky
Lodi
Long As I can See the Light
Lookin' Out My Backdoor
Proud Mary
Up Around the Bend
Run Through the Jungle
Sweet Hitch Hiker
Travelin' Band
Who'll Stop the Rain

Crosby, Stills, Nash and Young:
Carry On
Chicago
Love the One You're With
Ohio

Crosby, Stills, Nash and Young (Cont):
Our House
Suite Judy Blue Eyes
Teach Your Children
Woodstock
Helpless

Crowded House:
Don't Dream it's Over

The Cure:
Boys Don't Cry
Friday I'm in Love
Just Like Heaven
Lovesong

Cyndi Lauper:
Girls Just Wanna Have Fun
Time After Time

Cyprus Hill:
How I Could Just Kill A Man
Insane in the Membrane

D

The Dandy Warhol's:
Bohemian Like You
Cool Scene
Country Leaver
Godless
Horse Pills
Shakin'
Solid

The Dave Clark 5:
Bits & Pieces
Catch Us If You Can
Do You Love Me
Glad All Over

Dave Edmunds:
I Hear You Knocking

Dave Matthews Band:
Ants Marching
Crash into Me
Everyday
Gravedigger
Satellite
So Much to Say
The Space Between
Tripping Billies
What Would You Say
Where Are You Going

David Bowie:
Changes
Dancing In the Streets
Fame
Heroes
Let's Dance
Modern Love
Moonage Daydream
Rebel Rebel
Space Oddity
Starman
Suffragette City
The Jean Genie
Under Pressure
Young Americans
Ziggy Stardust

David Gilmour:
Murder

Days of the New:
Shelf in the Room
Touch, Peel and Stand

Dead or Alive:
You Spin Me Round (Like a Record)

The Dead Weather:
Are Friends Electric
Hang You from the Heavens

The Dead 60's:
Ghost Faced Killer
Riot Radio

The Decemberist:
O Valencia
Sixteen Military Wives
The Engine Driver
The Hazards of Love 1
The Rake's Song
Won't Want for Love (Margaret
    in the Taiga)

Deep Purple:
Highway Star
Hush
Lazy
Pictures of Home
Smoke on the Water
Space Truckin'
Woman from Tokyo

Def Leppard:
Armageddon It
Foolin'
Hysteria
Photograph
Pour Some Sugar on Me
Rock of Ages

Depeche Mode:
Enjoy the Silence
Just Can't Get Enough
People are People
Personal Jesus

Derek and the Dominos:
Bell Bottom Blues
Layla

Devo:
Mongoloid
Whip It

Dexy's Midnight Runners:
Come on Eileen

Dick Dale and the Del-Tones:
Miserlou
Nitro
Pipeline

Dire Straits:
Money for Nothing
Romeo and Juliet
Sultans of Swing
Walk of Life

The Distillers:
Beat Your Heart Out
City of Angles
Young Crazy Peeling

Donavan:
Catch the Wind
Colours
Hurdy Gurdy
Mellow Yellow
Sunshine Superman
The Universal Soldier

Donny Hathaway:
A Song for You

89 Great Guitar Songs and Riffs

1. Smoke On The Water - Deep Purple
2. Johnny B Goode - Chuck Berry
3. Sunshine Of Your Love - Cream
4. Layla - Derek And The Dominos
5. Whole Lotta Love - Led Zeppelin
6. Iron Man - Black Sabbath
7. Oh Pretty Woman - Roy Orbison
8. Stairway to Heaven – Led Zeppelin
9. You Really Got Me - The Kinks
10. Purple Haze - Jimi Hendrix Experience
11. Sweet Child O' Mine - Guns N' Roses
12. Whipping Post - Allman Brothers Band
13. (I Can't Get No) Satisfaction - The Rolling Stones
14. Walk This Way - Aerosmith
15. Wild Thing - The Troggs
16. Crossroads – Cream
17. Sweet Home Alabama - Lynyrd Skynyrd
18. Voodoo Chile (Slight Return) - Jimi Hendrix Experience
19. Paranoid - Black Sabbath
20. Crazy Train - Ozzy Osbourne
21. Back In Black - AC/DC
22. Foxy Lady - Jimi Hendrix Experience
23. Day Tripper - The Beatles
24. Aqualung - Jethro Tull
25. Bad To The Bone - George Thorogood & Destroyers
26. Brown Sugar - The Rolling Stones
27. Killing In The Name Of - Rage Against The Machine
28. Money For Nothing - Dire Straits
29. Jumpin' Jack Flash - The Rolling Stones
30. American Woman - The Guess Who
31. Kashmir - Led Zeppelin
32. Smells Like Teen Spirit - Nirvana

33. Black Dog - Led Zeppelin
34. Rebel Rebel - David Bowie
35. Roadhouse Blues - The Doors
36. Bo Diddley - Bo Diddley
37. Interstellar Overdrive - Pink Floyd
38. Runnin' With The Devil - Van Halen
39. Hells Bells - AC/DC
40. La Grange - ZZ Top
41. Sultans Of Swing - Dire Straits
42. N.I.B. - Black Sabbath
43. Pinball Wizard - The Who
44. Ace Of Spades - Motorhead
45. Wipeout - The Surfaris
46. Paradise City - Guns N' Roses
47. Don't Fear The Reaper - Blue Oyster Cult
48. All Day And All Of The Night - The Kinks
49. Bulls On Parade - Rage Against The Machine
50. All Along The Watchtower - Jimi Hendrix Experience
51. Are You Gonna Go My Way - Lenny Kravitz
52. Pride And Joy - Stevie Ray Vaughan
53. Statesboro Blues – Allman Brothers Band
54. Breaking The Law - Judas Priest
55. You Shook Me All Night Long - AC/DC
56. Rockin' In The Free World - Neil Young
57. Taxman - The Beatles
58. Panama – Van Halen
59. Over Under Sideways Down - The Yardbirds
60. Thunderstruck - AC/DC
61. Frankenstein - Edgar Winter
62. Miserlou – Dick Dale
63. Peace Frog – The Doors
64. My Generation – The Who
65. Bohemian Like You – The Dandy Warhol's
66. Blitzkrieg Bop – The Ramones
67. Seven Nation Army – The White Stripes
68. Molly's Chamber – Kings of Leon
69. Heartbreaker - Led Zeppelin

70. December – Collective Soul
71. Summertime Blues – Blue Cheer
72. Can't You Hear Me Knocking – The Rolling Stones
73. Black Magic Woman - Santana
74. I Can See for Miles – The Who
75. While My Guitar Gently Weeps - The Beatles
76. Born to Run – Bruce Springsteen
77. Cinnamon Girl – Neil Young
78. Eruption – Van Halen
79. White Room - Cream
80. Revolution – The Beatles
81. Free Bird – Lyrnyrd Skynyrd
82. American Girl – Tom Petty and the Heartbreakers
83. (We're Gonna) Rock Around the Clock – Bill Haley and His Comets
84. 1969 – The Stooges
85. Marquee Moon - Television
86. Omaha – Moby Grape
87. For What It's Worth – Buffalo Springfield
88. Summertime Blues –Eddie Cochran
89. Honey Don't – Carl Perkins

The Donnas:
Get Rid of the Girl
Take it Off

Don McLean:
American Pie

Doobie Brothers:
Black Water
China Grove
Listen to the Music

The Doors:
Alabama Song (Whisky Bar)
Back Door Man
Break on Through (To the Other
    Side)
Changeling
Five to One
Hello, I Love You
Hyacinth House
Land Ho!
LA Woman
Light My Fire
Love Her Madly
Love Me Two Times
Moonlight Drive
Peace Frog
People Are Strange
Riders on the Storm
Roadhouse Blues
Soul Kitchen
Take It As It Comes
The End
The Unknown Soldier
Touch Me

The Doors (Cont):
Twentieth Century Fox
Unhappy Girl
When the Music's Over
You're Lost Little Girl

Doyle Bramhall II:
Green Light Girl
Smokestack

Dragonforce:
Operation Ground and Pound
Through the Fires and Flames

Drowning Pool:
Bodies

Duane Eddy:
Peter Gunn
Rebel Rouser

Duffy:
Mercy
Warwick Avenue

Duran Duran:
Girls on Film
Hungry Like the Wolf
Is There Something I Should
    Know
Rio

Dusty Springfield
Son of a Preacher Man

E

The Eagles:
Heartache Tonight
Hotel California
Life in the Fast Lane
Take it Easy

Easy Beats:
Friday on My Mind
She's so Fine

Eddie Cochran:
C'mon Everybody
Summer Time Blues
Twenty Flight Rock

Edgar Winter Group:
Frankenstein
Free Ride

Edwin Starr:
War

Electric Light Orchestra:
Can't Get You Out Of My Head
Don't Bring Me Down
Do Ya
Eldorado Overture
Evil Woman
Roll Over Beethoven
Strange Magic

Elliot Smith:
A Distorted Reality is a Necessity
   to be Free
Miss Misery
Riot Coming

Elton John:
Candle in the Wind
Daniel
Don't Let the Sun Go Down On
   Me
Levon
Mona Lisas and Mad Hatters
Rocket Man
Sorry Seems To Be the Hardest
   Word
Tiny Dancer
Your Song

Elvis:
A Little Less Conversation
All Shook Up
Blue Suede Shoes
Can't Help Falling in Love
Don't Be Cruel
Heartbreak Hotel
Hound Dog
Jail House Rock
Mystery Train
Suspicious Minds
That's All Right

Elvis Costello:
Pump It Up
Radio Radio
(What's so Funny 'Bout) Peace
   Love and Understanding?

Emerson, Lake & Palmer:
From The Beginning
Hoedown
Jermy Bender/ The Sheriff
Karn Evil 9
a)   1st Impression
b)   2nd Impression
c)   3rd Impression
Lucky Man
Still … You Turn Me On
Nutrocker

Eric Clapton:
After Midnight
Cocaine
I Shot the Sheriff
Lay Down Sally
Layla (unplugged)
Let It Rain
Promises
She's Waiting
Tears in Heaven
Wonderful Tonight

Etta James:
At Last
I Just Wanna Make Love to You
Tell Mama

Eurythmics:
Here Comes the Rain Again
Sweet Dreams (Are Made of
    These)

Everclear:
AM Radio
I Will Buy You a New Life
Santa Monica
Wonderful

Eve 6:
Here's to the Night
Inside Out
Leech
Promise

20 of the Greatest Frontmen of all Time

My definition of a frontman is a lead singer who doesn't usually play an instrument. Elvis was often seen with a guitar but he didn't always play it and sometimes it didn't even have strings on it

1. Elvis Presley
2. Roger Daltrey – The Who
3. Robert Plant – Led Zeppelin
4. Jim Morrison – The Doors
5. Freddie Mercury – Queen
6. James Brown
7. David Bowie
8. Steven Tyler - Aerosmith
9. Mick Jagger – Rolling Stones
10. Bono – U2
11. Bon Scott – AC/DC
12. Iggy Pop – The Stooges, Solo
13. Otis Redding
14. Ozzy Osbourne – Black Sabbath, Solo
15. David Lee Roth – Van Halen
16. Alice Cooper
17. Axl Rose – Guns N' Roses
18. Joey Ramone – The Ramones
19. Janis Joplin – Big Brother and the Holding Company
20. Tine Turner

F

The Faces:
I'm Losing You
Stay With Me

The Fall:
Dead Beat Descendant
Victoria

Fall Out Boy:
I Don't Care
Thnks fr th Mmrs

Faker:
Are You Magnetic?
Hurricane
This Heart Attack

Fastball:
Fire Escape
Out of My Head
Sooner or Later
The Way
You're an Ocean

Fatboy Slim:
Praise You
Right Here, Right Now
The Rockefeller Skank

Feist:
I Feel it All

Feist (Cont):
Mushaboom
Past in Present
1-2-3-4

The Flaming Lips:
Do You Realize
She Don't Use Jelly
Shine on Sweet Jesus
The Yeah Yeah Yeah Song
W.A.N.D.

The Fleet Foxes:
He Doesn't Know Why
Ragged Wood
White Winter Hymnal

Fleetwood Mac:
Go Your Own Way
Landslide
Oh Well

Flobots:
Handlebars
Rise

Flock of Seagulls:
I Ran (So Far Away)

Flogging Molly:
Black Friday Rule
Devil's Dance Floor
If I Ever Leave This World Alive
Seven Deadly Sins
Salty Dog

Flogging Molly (Cont):
The Likes of You Again
The Rare Old Times
What's Left of the Flag
Within a Mile of Home

The Fly's:
Got You Where I Want You

Filter:
Hey Man Nice Shot
Take a Picture

Finger Eleven:
One Thing

Fiona Apple:
Criminal

Five for Fighting:
Superman (It's not Easy)
100 Years

Five Man Electrical Band:
Signs

The Fixx:
One Thing Leads to Another

Foghat:
I Just Want To Make Love to You
Slow Ride

Folk Implosion:
Free to Go
Natural One

Fountains of Wayne:
Denise
Go, Hippie
I've Got a Flair
Joe Rey
Laser Show
Leave the Biker
Lost in Space
Radiation Vibe
Red Dragon Tattoo
Sink to the Bottom
Stacy's Mom
Troubled Times
Utopia Parkway

Frank Sinatra:
Fly Me to the Moon
Love and Marriage
My Way
New York New York
Strangers in the Night

Franz Ferdinand:
Take Me Out

The Fray:
How to Save a Life

Free:
All Right Now
Fire & Water

Foo Fighters:
Big Me
Everlong
Learn to Fly
Monkey Wrench
Next Year
This is a Call

The Fugees:
Killing Me Softly
No Woman No Cry

G

Garbage:
Only Happy When it Rains
Stupid Girl

Gary Numan:
Cars

Genesis:
Abacab
Follow You Follow Me
Home By The Sea
I Can't Dance
In the Air Tonight
Invisible Touch
Just a Job to Do
Misunderstanding
That's All
Tonight, Tonight, Tonight
Turn It On Again

George Harrison:
All Things Must Pass
Give Me Love
Got My Mind Set On You
My Sweet Lord

George Thorogood:
Bad to the Bone
Highway 49
I Drink Alone
Move it on Over
One Bourbon, One Scotch, One
    Beer

George Thorogood (Cont):
Ride on Josephine
Who Do You Love

Georgia Satellites:
Keep Your Hands to Yourself

Gin Blossoms:
Hey Jealousy
Follow You Down
Found Out About You

G. Love and Special Sauce:
Cold Beverages
Kiss and Tell
Peace, Love and Happiness
Soft and Sweet

The Go-Go's:
Our Lips are Sealed
Vacation
We Got the Beat

Gordon Lightfoot:
Sundown

Grand Funk Railroad:
We're an American Band
I'm Your Captain/Closer to
    Home (Medley)

**Grandmaster Flash and
The Furious 5:**
The Message

Grateful Dead:
Box of Rain
Casey Jones
Dark Star
Friend of the Devil
One More Saturday Night
St. Stephen
Touch of Grey
Truckin'
West L.A. Fade Away

Green Day:
American Idiot
Basket Case
Boulevard of Broken Dreams
Brain Stew
Burnout
Chump
Church on Sunday
Good Riddance (Time of Your Life)
Holiday
Jaded
Know Your Enemy
Macy's Day Parade
Minority
Prosthetic Head
She
Wake Me Up When September
    Ends
Walking Alone
Warning
Welcome to Paradise
When I Come Around
21ˢᵗ Century Breakdown

Greg Kihn Band:
The Breakup Song(They Don't
    Write 'Em)

Golden Earring:
Radar Love

Gorillaz:
Clint Eastwood
Dirty Harry

The Guess Who:
American Woman
Hand Me Down World
No Sugar Tonight/ New Mother
    Nature
No Time
Share the Land

Guided By Voices:
Game of Pricks
Glad Girls
I Am a Scientist
Teenage FBI

Guns N' Roses:
Civil War
Knockin' on Heaven's Door
Live and Let Die
Mr. Brownstone
November Rain
Paradise City
Patience
Sweet Child O' Mine
Welcome to the Jungle
You Could Be Mine

Best Guilty Pleasure Songs

The Go-Go's: Our Lips are Sealed, We Got the Beat

Avril Lavigne: Complicated

Nena: 99 Luftbaloons

The Archies: Sugar, Sugar

The Bangles: Walk Like an Egyptian

The B-52's: Love Shack, Rock Lobster

Cyndi Lauper: Girls Just Wanna Have Fun

Nancy Sinatra: These Boots are Made for Walking

The Proclaimers: (I'm Gonna Be) 500 Miles

Tommy Tutone: Jenny/867-5309

The Vapors: Turning Japanese

H

Hank Williams:
I'm So Lonesome I Could Cry
Your Cheatin' Heart

Harry Chapin:
Cat's in the Cradle
Taxi

Harvey Danger:
Flagpole Sitta

Hayes Carll:
It's a Shame

Heart:
Barracuda
Magic Man

Hey Monday:
Homecoming

The Hives:
Abra Cadaver
Broken Bones
Die Alright
Find Another Girl
Hate to Say I Told You So
Inspection Wise 1999
Main Offender
Supply and Demand

The Hives (Cont):
The Hives-Declare Guerre
    Nucleaire
Tick Tick Boom
Two Timing Touch
Walk Idiot Walk

Hole:
Celebrity Skin
Doll Parts

Hollies:
Bus Stop
Long Cool Woman (In a Black
    Dress)

The Hooters:
All You Zombies
And We Danced
Boys of Summer
Day by Day
Hanging On a Heart Beat
I'm Alive
South Ferry Road

Hootie and the Blowfish:
Hold My Hand
I Go Blind
Let Her Cry
Only Wanna be With You

House of Pain:
Jump Around

Howlin' Wolf:
Smoke Stack Lightning
Shake it for Me
Spoonful

Human League:
Don't You Want Me

Humble Pie:
Stone Cold Fever

Huey Lewis & The News:
I Want a New Drug
The Heart of Rock & Roll
The Power of Love
Workin For a Livin

Husker Du:
Could You Be the One
Don't Want to Know if You are
    Lonely
Makes No Sense at All

15 Great Blues Songs

Blues is the foundation that Rock N' Roll was built upon.

Robert Johnson: Cross Road Blues
                          Sweet Home Chicago

Led Belly: Where Did You Sleep Last Night

B.B. King: How Blue Can You Get
                          The Thrill Is Gone

Bukka White: Fixin' to Die Blues

Muddy Waters: Baby Please Don't Go
                          Got My Mojo Working
                          Mannish Boy

John Lee Hooker: Boom Boom
                          Dimples
                          One Bourbon, One Scotch, One Beer
                          Please Don't Go

Screamin' Jay Hawkins: I Put a Spell On You

Howlin' Wolf: Spoonful

I

Ice Cube:
It was a Good Day

Iggy Pop:
Lust for Life
Real Wild Child (Wild One)
Shoeshine Girl

Incubus:
Drive
I Wish You Were Here

INXS:
Don't Change
Need You Tonight
Never Tear Us Apart
New Sensation
Pretty Vegas

Iron Butterfly:
In-A-Gadda-Da-Vida

Iron Maiden:
Run to the Hills

The Isley Brothers:
Shout

Israel Kamakawiwo'ole:
Somewhere Over the Rainbow

J

Jack Johnson:
Better Together
Bubble Toes
Sitting, Waiting, Wishing
Upside Down

Jackson Browne:
Runnin on Empty

Jakob Dylan:
On Up the Mountain
Will it Grow

Jan and Dean:
Dead Man's Curve
Little Old Lady from Pasadena

The Jam:
A Town Called Malice
Eaton Rifles
Going Underground
That's Entertainment

James:
Laid
Sometimes

James Brown:
I Got You (I Feel Good)
Papa's Got a Brand New Bag

James Gang:
Funk #49
Seems to Be
Tend My Garden
The Bomber
a) Closet Queen
b) Cast Your Fate To The Walk Away
Wind
Woman

Jane's Addiction:
Been Caught Stealing
Jane Says

Janis Joplin (Big Brother and the Holding Company):
Ball and Chain
Down on Me
Cry Baby
Me and Bobby McGee

Mercedes Benz
Piece of My Heart
Summertime

The Jayhawks:
Bad Time
Blue
I'm Gonna Make You Love Me
Pray for Me

Jeff Beck (Group):
A Day in the Life
Amazing Grace
Freeway Jam
I Ain't Superstitious

Jeff Buckley:
Hallelujah

Jefferson Airplane:
Embryonic Journey
It's No Secret
Somebody to Love
Volunteers
White Rabbit

Jeff Healy Band:
I Think I Love You Too Much
I Tried

Jerry Lee Lewis:
Great Balls of Fire
Little Queenie
Whole Lotta Shakin' Goin On

The Jesus and Mary Chain:
April Skies
Darklands
Head On
Just Like Honey
Sometimes Always

Jet:
Are You Gonna be My Girl
Bring it on Back
Cold Hard Bitch
Hey Kids
Look What You've Done
Rip it Up
Rollover DJ
Shiny Magazine

Jethro Tull:
Aqualung
Bouree
Bungle in the Jungle
Living in The Past
Locomotive Breath
Teacher
Thick as a Brick
Witch's Promise

J. Geils Band:
Centerfold
I Do
Love Stinks

Jimi Hendrix:
All Along the Watchtower
Are You Experienced
Castles Made of Sand
Crosstown Traffic
Dolly Dagger
Fire
Foxy Lady
Freedom
Gloria
Here He Comes (Lover Man)
Hey Joe
Johnny B. Goode
Killing Floor
Like a Rolling Stone
Machine Gun
Purple Haze
Rock Me Baby
Star Spangled Banner
The Wind Cries Mary
Voodoo Child
Wild Thing

Jimmy Eat World:
Pain
Sweetness
The Middle

Jimmy's Chicken Shack:
Do Right

J.J Cale:
After Midnight
Call Me the Breeze
Cocaine
Down to Memphis
Oh Mary
Roll On

Joan Jett & The Blackhearts:
Bad Reputation
Cherry Bomb
Crimson and Clover
Do You Wanna Touch
Fake Friends
I Love Rock n' Roll

Joe Cocker:
Feeling Alright
She Came in Through the
     Bathroom Window
With a Little Help From My
     Friends
You Are So Beautiful

Joe Jackson:
Breaking Us in Two
Is She Really Going Out With Him
Steppin' Out

Joe Walsh:
Life's Been Good
Rocky Mountain Way

John Denver:
Take Me Home, Country Roads

John Fogerty:
Centerfield

John Lee Hooker:
Boom Boom
Dimples
Leave My Wife Alone
One Bourbon, One Scotch, One
     Beer
Please Don't Go

John Lennon:
Happy X-Mas (War is Over)
Instant Karma
Imagine
Stand By Me
Watching the Wheels
Whatever Gets You Thru the
     Night
Working Class Hero

23 of the Greatest Guitarist of all Time

1. Jimi Hendrix - The Jimi Hendrix Experience, Band of Gypsies

2. Jimmy Page - Led Zeppelin

3. Eric Clapton -Yardbirds, Cream, Derek & The Dominos, Blind Faith, Solo

4. Pete Townshend - The Who

5. Jeff Beck - Yardbirds, Jeff Beck Group, Solo

6. Duane Allman - Allman Brothers Band, Derek & The Dominos

7. Eddie Van Halen - Van Halen

8. Stevie Ray Vaughan - Stevie Ray Vaughan & Double Trouble

9. Ritchie Blackmore - Deep Purple, Rainbow, Blackmores Night

10. Carlos Santana - Santana

11. Tony Iommi - Black Sabbath

12. Mark Knopfler - Dire Straits, Solo

13. Slash - Guns N' Roses, Velvet Revolver

14. Tom Morello - Rage Against the Machine, Audioslave

15. George Harrison – The Beatles, Traveling Wilburys, Solo

16. Brian May - Queen

17. Steve Miller – Steve Miller Band

18. Angus Young - AC/DC

19. Keith Richards - Rolling Stones

20. Chuck Berry - Solo

21. David Gilmour – Pink Floyd

22. Joe Perry - Aerosmith

23. Jack White – The White Stripes

John Mellencamp:
Crumblin' Down
Paper in Fire
Hurts so Good
I Need a Lover
Jack and Diane
Lonely Ol' Night
Pink Houses
Small Town

Johnny Cash:
A Boy Named Sue
Cocaine Blues
Cry Cry Cry
Delia's Gone
Don't Take Your Guns to Town
Folsom Prison Blues
Get Rhythm
God's Gonna Cut You Down
Hey Porter
Hurt
I Still Miss Someone
I've Been Everywhere
I Walk the Line
Jackson
Man in Black
Ring of Fire
Sunday Morning Coming Down
The Man Comes Around
The Night Hank Williams Came
    to Town
What Do I Care
25 Minutes to Go

Jorma Kaukonen:
Blue Railroad Train
Embryonic Journey
Hesitation Blues

Journey:
Any Way You Want It
Don't Stop Believin'
Lovin', Touchin', Squeezin'
Wheel in The Sky

JR. Walker:
Shotgun

Judas Priest:
Breaking the Law
You've Got Another Thing
    Comin'

K

Kaiser Chiefs:
Everything is Average Nowdays
Good Days Bad Days
I Predict a Riot
Never Miss a Beat
Ruby

Kansas:
Carry on Wayward Son
Dust in the Wind

Kanye West:
Gold Digger

Kenny Wayne Shepherd:
Blue on Black

Kid Rock:
All Summer Long
Amen
American Bad Ass
Bawitdaba
Cowboy
Only God Knows Why
Picture
Wasting Time

The Killers:
All These Things That I've Done
Human
Mr. Brightside
Read My Mind

The Killers (Cont):
Romeo and Juliet
Shadowplay
Somebody Told Me
Spaceman
When You Were Young

The Kills:
Cheap and Cheerful
Good Ones
Last Day of Magic

Kimya Dawson:
I Like Giants
Loose Lips
So Nice so Smart
Time to Think
Tire Swing
Tree Hugger

King Crimson:
The Court of the Crimson King
a) The Return of the Fire Watch
b) The Dance of the Puppets
Indiscipline
21st Century Schizoid Man

Kings of Leon:
Happy Alone
Holy Roller Novocain
Joe's Head
Molly's Chamber
Notion
On Call
Red Morning Light
Sex on Fire
The Bucket
Use Somebody

The Kingsmen:
Louie Louie

The Kinks:
All Day and All of the Night
A Well Respected Man
Catch Me Now I'm Falling
Celluloid Heroes
Come Dancing
I'm Not Like Everybody Else
Lola
State Of Confusion
Sunny Afternoon
Supersonic Rocket Ship
Tired Of Waiting for You
Till The End of the Day
Waterloo Sunset
Wish I Could Fly Like Superman
You Really Got Me

Kiss:
Detroit Rock City
Rock and Roll All Night (and
    Party Every Day)

The Knack:
Good Girls Don't
My Sharona

The Knux:
Bang Bang

Kooks:
Always Where I Need to Be
Belly Love
California

Kooks (Cont):
Naive
Ooh La
Seaside
She Moves in Her Own Way
Shine On

Korn:
Freak on a Leash

KRS One:
You Must Learn

L

The Last Shadow Puppets:
My Mistakes Were Made For You
Standing Next to Me
The Age of the Understatement

Led Belly:
Pick a Bale of Cotton
Where Did You Sleep Last Night

Led Zeppelin:
All My Love
Babe I'm Gonna Leave You
Black Dog
Bonzo's Montreux
Bron-y-aur Stomp
Communication Breakdown
Dancing Days
Darlene
D'yer Maker
Dazed and Confused
Fool in the Rain
Four Sticks
Friends
Gallows Pole
Going to California
Good Times Bad Times
Heartbreaker/Living Loving
   Maid (She's Just a Woman)
Hey Hey What Can I Do
Houses of the Holy
How Many More Times
Immigrant Song

Led Zeppelin (Cont):
In the Evening
Kashmir
Misty Mountain Hop
Moby Dick
Nobody's Fault but Mine
Over the Hills and Far Away
Poor Tom
Ramble On
Rock N' Roll
South Bound Suarez
Stairway to Heaven
Tangerine
Thank You
That's the Way
The Battle of Evermore
The Ocean
The Rain Song
The Song Remains the Same
The Wanton Song
What is and What Should Never
   Be
When the Levee Breaks
Whole Lotta Love

The Lemon Heads:
Mrs. Robinson

Len:
If You Steal My Sunshine

Lenny Kravitz:
American Woman
Are You Gonna Go My Way
Fly Away

Leon Russell:
Jumping Jack Flash/Youngblood
    Medley
Mighty Quinn Medley
a.) I'll Take You There
b.) Idol with the Golden Hand
c.) I Serve a Living Savior
d.) Mighty Quinn

Less Than Jake:
Help Save the Youth of America
    from Exploding

The Libertines:
Can't Stand Me Now
Don't Look Back into the Sun
Time for Heroes
Up the Bracket

Lit:
Down
Four
My Own Worst Enemy
Zip-Lock

Little Richard:
Good Golly, Miss Molly
Tutti-Fruitti

Live:
I Alone
Lightning Crashes

Living Colour:
Cult of Personality

The Living End:
Roll On

Liz Phair:
6'1"
Divorce Song
Fuck and Run
Help Me Marry
Never Said
Soap Star Joe
Why Can't I Breathe

L.L. Cool J:
Momma Said Knock You Out

Local H:
All the Kids Are Right
Bound for the Floor

Long Beach Dub All-Stars:
Sunny Hours

Louis Armstrong:
Dream a Little Dream of Me
What a Wonderful World

Lou Reed:
Rock and Roll
Sweet Jane
Walk on the Wild Side

15 of the Greatest Drummers of all Time

1. John Bonham – Led Zeppelin

2. Keith Moon – The Who

3. Ginger Baker – Cream, Blind Faith

4. Neil Peart – Rush

5. Mitch Mitchell – The Jimi Hendrix Experience

6. Buddy Rich – Big Band and Jazz session drummer

7. Bill Ward – Black Sabbath

8. Carl Palmer – Emerson, Lake and Palmer

9. Ian Paice – Deep Purple

10. John Densmore – The Doors

11. Nick Mason – Pink Floyd

12. Alex Van Halen – Van Halen

13. Bill Bruford – Yes, King Crimson

14. Ringo Starr – The Beatles

15. Jim Keltner – Studio/Session Drummer

The Lovin' Spoonful:
Do You Believe in Magic
Summer in the City

Lynyrd Skynyrd:
Call Me the Breeze
Free Bird
Gimme Three Steps
Saturday Night Special
Simple Man
Sweet Home Alabama
That Smell
What's Your Name

20 Great Drum Songs

1. Moby Dick – Led Zeppelin
2. Won't Get Fooled Again - The Who
3. Toad - Cream
4. Rock N' Roll – Led Zeppelin
5. 21st Century Schizoid Man - King Crimson
6. La Villa Strangiato - Rush
7. Soul Sacrifice - Santana
8. In A Gadda Da Vida - Iron Butterfly
9. Who Are You – The Who
10. Karn Evil 9 – Emerson, Lake & Palmer
11. Hot for Teacher – Van Halen
12. Indiscipline – King Crimson
13. Fire – Jimi Hendrix
14. Space Truckin - Deep Purple
15. War Pigs – Black Sabbath
16. Four Sticks – Led Zeppelin
17. Wipe Out - Surfaris
18. My Generation – The Who
19. White Room - Cream
20. Lust for Life – Iggy Pop

M

Madness:
Our House

The Mamas and the Papas:
California Dreamin'
Dream a Little Dream of Me
Monday, Monday

Manfred Mann (Earth Band):
Blinded by the Light
Do Wah Diddy
Mighty Quinn (Quinn the Eskimo)

Marcy Playground:
Poppies
Saint Joe on the School Bus
Sex and Candy

Mark Knopfler:
Why Aye Man
What it is

Mark Olson:
Bicycle
Bloody Hands
Chamberlain, SD
Clifton Bridge
Doves and Stones
Life's Warm Sheets

Marshall Tucker Band:
Can't You See

Martha and the Vandellas:
Nowhere to Run
Dancing in the Streets

Marvin Gaye:
Ain't No Mountain High Enough
What's Going On

Matchbox 20:
How Far We've Come
If You're Gone
Push
3am

Matt Costa:
Cold December
Lilacs
Miss Magnolia
Mr. Pitiful
Sunshine
Sweet Thursday
Unfamiliar Faces

Matthew Sweet:
Come to California
Divine Intervention
Sick of Myself
We're the Same

MC5:
American Ruse
Baby Won't Ya
Kick Out the Jams
Looking at You

Meat Loaf:
You Took the Words Right Out
    Of My Mouth

Meat Puppets:
Backwater
Lake of Fire
Oh Me
Plateau

Me First and the Gimme Gimmes:
Goodbye Earl
I Believe I Can Fly
Rainbow Conection

Megadeth:
Breadline

Men Without Hats:
Safety Dance

Men at Work:
Be Good Johnny
Down Under
Who Can It Be Now

Metallica:
Enter Sandman
Master of Puppets

Metro Station:
Shake It

MGMT:
Electric Feel
Kids
Time to Pretend

Midnight Oil:
Beds Are Burning

The Mighty Mighty Boss Tones:
So Sad to Say
That Bug Bit Me
The Impression That I Get
The Rascal King
Where You Come From

Mitch Ryder and the Detroit Wheels:
Devil With a Blue Dress On/
    Good Golly Miss Molly
Jenny Take a Ride

Moby:
Bodyrock
Natural Blues
Porcelain
Run On
South Side
We Are All Made of Stars

Moby Grape:
Ain't No Use
Ain't That a Shame
Changes
Fall on You

Moby Grape (Cont):
Hey Grandma
Omaha
Sweet Ride

Modern English:
Melt With You

Modest Mouse:
Dashboard
Float On
Ocean Breathes Salty
The World at Large

The Moldy Peaches:
Anyone Else But You
Who's Got the Crack

Moody Blues:
Go Now
I'm Just a Singer (In a Rock and
    Roll Band)
Nights in White Satin
Question
Ride My See-Saw
Tuesday Afternoon

Mooney Suzuki:
Alive and Amplified
Electric Sweat
Half of My Heart
In a Young Man's Mind
Shake that Bush Again
This Broken Heart of Mine
99%

Motorhead:
Ace of Spades
Born to Raise Hell

Mott the Hoople:
All the Way to Memphis
All the Young Dudes
Honaloochie Boogie
Sweet Jane

Mountain:
Mississippi Queen

Mudcrutch:
Lover on the Bayou
Scare Easy

Muddy Waters:
Baby Please Don't Go
Got My Mojo Working
Hoochie Coochie Man
Mannish Boy
Rollin Stone

The Murmurs:
La Di Da
White Rabbit
You Suck

My Bloody Valentine:
Only Shallow
Sometimes-Lost in Translation
Soon
To Here Knows When
You Made Me Realize

My Chemical Romance:
The Black Parade

My Morning Jacket:
Off the Record

Muse:
Hysteria

M. Ward:
Carolina
Chinese Translation
Epistemology
Half Moon
Jailbird
Never Had Anybody Like You
One Hundred Million Years
Requiem
To Go Home
Vincent O'Brien
Were You There

N

Nada Surf:
Popular

Nancy Sinatra:
These Boots are Made for
    Walking

Nas:
Hip Hop is Dead
I Know I Can

The National:
Apartment Story
Mistaken for Strangers
Slow Show

Naughty by Nature:
Hip Hop Hooray

Nazz:
Hang on Paul
Hello It's Me
Not Wrong Long
Open My Eyes
You Sexy Thing

Nena:
99 Luftbaloons

Neil Young:
After The Goldrush
Cinnamon Girl
Cowgirl in the Sand
Don't Let It Bring You Down
Down by the River
Heart of Gold
Helpless
Long May You Run
Mr. Soul
My My Hey Hey
Ohio
Old Man
Rockin' in the Free World
Sugar Mountain
Southern Man
The Needle and the Damage
    Done

New Order:
Blue Monday

The New Radicals:
You Get What You Give

New York Dolls:
Chatterbox
Looking for a Kiss
Personality Crisis
Pills
Trash

Nick Drake:
From the Morning
Pink Moon
Three Hours

Nick Lowe:
Cruel to be Kind
Half a Boy and Half a Man
So it Goes

Nickleback:
Rockstar

Nine Inch Nails:
Fuck You Like an Animal

Nirvana:
About a Girl
All Apologies
Aneurysm
Been a Son
Come As You Are
Dumb
Heart-Shaped Box
In Bloom
Jesus Don't Want Me for a
    Sunbeam
Lake of Fire
Lithium
Man Who Sold the World
Molly's Lips
Pennyroyal Tea
Plateau
Rape Me
Serve the Servants
Smells Like Teen Spirit
Turnaround
Where Did You Sleep Last Night
You Know You're Right

No Doubt:
Don't Speak
Just a Girl

Norman Greenbaum:
Spirit in the Sky

27 Club

A number of musicians have died when they were 27 years old. Some refer to it as the 27 Club, some call it Robert Johnson's Curse. Whatever you want to call it, these are the unfortunate musicians who died when they were only 27 years old.

Robert Johnson	August 16, 1938	Blues Singer
Rudy Lewis	May 20, 1964	The Drifters
Brian Jones	July 3, 1969	The Rolling Stones
Alan Wilson	September 3, 1970	Canned Heat
Jimi Hendrix	September 18, 1970	
Janis Joplin	October 4, 1970	
Jim Morrison	July 3, 1971	The Doors
Ron McKernan	March 8, 1973	The Grateful Dead
Dave Alexander	February 10, 1975	The Stooges
Peter Ham	April 24, 1975	Badfinger
Chris Bell	December 27, 1978	Big Star
Kurt Cobain	April 5, 1994	Nirvana
Kristen Pfaff	June 16, 1994	Hole

Only the Good Die Young

Billy Joel once sang, "Only the good die young" and maybe that's true. Here is a list of some of the other musicians who died entirely too young. Along with those in the 27 Club, it leaves music lovers wondering what other great music could they have produced had they lived longer.

Muscian	Age	Band
Richie Valens	17	Solo
Eddie Cochran	21	Solo
Sid Vicious	21	The Sex Pistols
Buddy Holly	22	Buddy Holly and the Crickets
Duane Allman	24	The Allman Brothers Band
Berry Oakley	24	The Allman Brothers Band
Cliff Burton	24	Metallica
The Notorious B.I.G.	24	Rapper
Randy Rhoads	25	Ozzy Osbourne
Tupac Shakur	25	Rapper
Otis Redding	26	Solo
Hillel Slovak	26	The Red Hot Chili Peppers
Shannon Hoon	28	Blind Mellon
Bradley Nowell	28	Sublime
Ronnie Van Zant	29	Lynyrd Skynyrd
Jeff Buckley	30	Solo
Terry Kath	31	Chicago
John Bonham	32	Led Zeppelin
Keith Moon	32	The Who
Bon Scott	33	AC/DC
Bob Marley	36	Bob Marley and the Wailers
Michael Hutchence	37	INXS
Dennis Dannell	38	Social Distortion
John Lennon	40	The Beatles/Solo
Elvis Presley	42	Solo
Marvin Gaye	44	Solo
Freddie Mercury	45	Queen

O

Oasis:
Champagne Supernova
Don't Go Away
Don't Look Back in Anger
D'you Know What I Mean
Fade In-Out
Going Nowhere
Go Let it Out
Half the World Away
Headshrinker
I Am the Walrus
Little James
Live Forever
Lord Don't Slow Me Down
Rockin' Chair
Rock N' Roll Star
Roll With It
Shakermaker
Stop Crying Your Heart Out
Supersonic
The Shock and the Lightning
Who Feels Love
Wonderwall

The Offspring:
Come Out and Play
Self-Esteem
She's Got Issues
The Kids Aren't Alright
Why Don't You Get a Job

Ok Go:
A Good Idea at the Time
Don't Ask Me
Do What You Want
Get Over It
Here it Goes Again
Invincible
Let it Rain
Television, Television
There's a Fire

Old Crow Medicine Show:
Down Home Girl
I Hear Them All
Tell it to Me
Wagon Wheel

OMC:
How Bizarre

One Republic:
Apologize
Mercy
Stop an Stare

Otis Redding:
Respect
Satisfaction
Shake
(Sittin' on) The Dock of the Bay

Outkast:
Hey Ya

The Outfield:
Your Love

Ozzy Osbourne:
Crazy Train
Mama I'm Coming Home

P

Panic at the Disco:
Nine in the Afternoon

The Panics:
Don't Fight It

Patsy Cline:
Crazy
I Fall to Pieces

The Paul Butterfield Blues Band:
Look Over Yonders Wall
Mellow Down Easy

Paul McCartney (Wings):
Band on the Run
Hi Hi Hi
Jet
Junior's Farm
Let 'em In
Live and Let Die
London Town
Maybe I'm Amazed
Venus and Mars/Rock Show

Pete Townshend:
Give Me a Heart to Hang On To
Greyhound Girl
Let My Love Open the Door

Pete Townshend (Con't):
Sheraton Gibson
There's Heartache Following Me

Peter Gabriel:
Big Time
Games Without Frontiers
In Your Eyes
Shock the Monkey
Sledgehammer
Solsbury Hill

Pet Shop Boys:
Always on My Mind

Petula Clark:
Downtown

Pearl Jam(Eddie Vedder):
Alive
Better Man
Black
Daughter
Even Flow
Far Behind
Guaranteed
Hard Sun
I Believe in Miracles
Jeremy
Love Reign O'er Me
The Patriot
Porch
Rise
Tuolumne
Wish List
Worldwide Suicide

Peter Frampton:
All I Want To Be (Is By Your Side)
Baby I Love Your Way
Do You Feel Like We Do
Show Me the Way

Pete Yorn:
Life on a Chain
Strange Condition

Phantom Planet:
California

Phil Collins:
I Don't Care Anymore
In the Air Tonight
Sussudio
You Can't Hurry Love
You'll Be In My Heart

Phil Phillips:
Sea of Love

Pink Floyd:
Another Brick in the Wall part 2
Astronomy Domine
Brain Damage/Eclipse
Breathe
Comfortably Numb
Dogs
Echoes
Have a Cigar
Hey You
Interstellar Overdrive

Pink Floyd (Cont):
Learning to Fly
Money
Mother
One of These Days
On The Turning Away
Pigs
See Emily Play
Sheep
Shine on You Crazy Diamond
    (Parts 1-7)
The Dogs of War
Time
Us and Them
Welcome To the Machine
Wish You Were Here

The Pixies:
Debaser
Here Comes Your Man
Monkey Gone to Heaven

PJ Harvey:
Good Fortune
This is Love

Plain White T's:
Hey There Delilah

The Police:
Every Breath You Take
Every Little Thing She Does is
    Magic

The Police (Cont):
Don't Stand so Close to Me
Message in a Bottle
Roxanne

**The Presidents of the
United States of America:**
Lump
Peaches

Pretenders:
Back On the Chain Gang
Brass in Pocket
Middle of the Road

Primitive Radio Gods:
Standing Outside a Broken
    Phone Booth

The Proclaimers:
(I'm Gonna Be) 500 Miles

Public Enemy:
Bring the Noise
Fight the Power

Public Image Limited:
Rise

Puddle of Mudd:
Psycho
She Hates Me

Pure Prairie League:
Amie

When buying records I used to have one simple rule, the album had to have at least three songs that I liked or I wouldn't buy it. In recent years the album has been a dying art form. First, CD's made it easy to skip over the songs that you didn't like and program in just the songs that you wanted to listen to. Now, with computers you can download just the songs you want without buying the album. With this latest technology there seems to be a growing trend among new bands that rather than putting out a full album of material they focus on putting out singles. This is nothing new. Early on record companies used to sell 45's with maybe two tracks per side. It wasn't until the Beatles that full length albums (LP's) became the norm. It's too soon to know whether or not the return of singles is here to stay or if we will see another shift back to full length albums. While we wait here are some albums that every music lover should have.

Albums That Everyone Should Own

The Beatles: Revolver, Abby Road, Sgt. Pepper

The Who: Tommy, Who's Next

Pink Floyd: Dark Side of the Moon, The Wall

Led Zeppelin: I, II, III, IV

Jimi Hendrix: Are You Experienced, Electric Ladyland

The Rolling Stones: Exile On Main Street, Let It Bleed

The Doors: The Doors

The Beach Boys: Pet Sounds

Nirvana: Nevermind, Unplugged

U2: The Joshua Tree, Achtung Baby

Sex Pistols: Never Mind the Bollocks

AC/DC: Back in Black

Bob Dylan: Blonde on Blonde, Highway 61 Revisited

The Clash: London Calling

Bruce Springsteen: Born To Run

Cream: Disraeli Gears

The Ramones: The Ramones

Black Sabbath: Paranoid, Black Sabbath

David Bowie: Ziggy Stardust

Green Day: Dookie, American Idiot

Q

Queen:
Another One Bites the Dust
Bohemian Rhapsody
Crazy Little Thing Called Love
Fat Bottom Girls
Keep Yourself Alive
Killer Queen
Now I'm Here
Radio Ga Ga
Somebody to Love
Under Pressure
You're My Best Friend
We Are the Champions
We Will Rock You

Queensberry:
No Smoke

Queens of the Stone Age:
No One Knows

Quicksilver Messenger Service:
Dino's Song
Mona
Pride of Man

Best Christmas/Holiday Songs:

Bruce Springsteen – Santa Clause is Coming to Town

The Kinks – Father Christmas

The Waitresses- Christmas Wrapping

Chuck Berry – Run Run Rudolph

John Lennon – Happy Xmas

Tom Petty- Christmas All Over Again

The Beach Boys - Little St. Nick

The Who - Christmas

Ted Nugent – Deck the Halls

Emerson, Lake and Palmer – I Believe in Father Christmas

Band Aid – Do They Know It's Christmas?

R

The Raconteurs:
Broken Boy Soldier
Hands
Level
Steady as She Goes

Radiohead:
Creep
Fake Plastic Trees
High and Dry
My Iron Lung
Optimistic
Paranoid Android
Thinking About You

Rage Against the Machine:
Bulls on Parade
Freedom
Guerilla Radio
How I Could Just Kill a Man
Killing in the Name of
People of the Sun
Renegades of Funk
Sleep Now in the Fire
Testify
Wake Up

Ramones:
Blitzkrieg Bop
California Sun
I Believe in Miracles
I Wanna be Sedated

Ramones (Cont):
R.A.M.O.N.E.S.
Rock 'N' Roll High School
Sheena is a Punk Rocker
She's A Sensation
She Talks to Rainbows
Swallow My Pride
Teenage Lobotomy
The KKK Took My Baby Away
What a Wonderful World

The Rascals:
Freakbeat Phantom
I'll Give You My Sympathy
Out of Dreams
Suspicious Wit

Ray Charles:
Georgia on My Mind
Hit the Road Jack
I Got Woman
Shake Your Tailfeather
What'd I Say

Ray LaMontagne:
Be Here Now
Henry Nearly Killed Me (It's a
    Shame)
Three More Days
Trouble

The Red Hot Chili Peppers:
Breaking the Girl
Californication
Dani California
Give it Away

The Red Hot Chili Peppers (Cont):
Higher Ground
Love Rollercoaster
Scar Tissue
Under the Bridge

Reel Big Fish:
Sell Out

R.E.M.:
Bad Day
Day Sleeper
Drive
Everybody Hurts
Imitation of Life
It's the End of the World as We
    Know it (And I Feel Fine)
Losing My Religion
Man on the Moon
Orange Crush
Radio Free Europe
Shiny Happy People
Stand
Superman
Supernatural Superserious
The One I Love
What's the Frequency, Kenneth

The Replacements:
Bastards of Young
Can't Hardly Wait
I Will Dare
Unsatisfied

Ringo Starr:
It Don't Come Easy
Photograph

Richie Havens:
Freedom
Here Comes the Sun
License to Kill

Ritchie Valens:
Come On, Let's Go
Donna
La Bamba

Rob Base and DJ E-Z Rock:
It Takes Two

Robert Johnson:
Cross Road Blues
Sweet Home Chicago

Robert Palmer:
Addicted to Love
Bad Case of Loving You
Simply Irresistible

Robert Plant:
Skip's Song

Robert Plant with Allison Krauss:
Gone, Gone, Gone
Rich Women
Stick with Me Baby

Robert Randolph and The Family Band:
Ain't Nothing Wrong With That
Don't Stop 'Til You Get Enough
I Need More Love

Robyn Hitchcock and the Egyptians:
Man with the Lightbulb Head
So You Think You're in Love

Rod Stewart:
Downtown Train
Every Picture Tells a Story
Forever Young
Maggie May
Ooh La La
Reason to Believe
Stay With Me
The First Cut is the Deepest
The Motown Song
Young Turks
You're in My Heart
You Wear It Well

Rob Zombie (White Zombie):
Dragula
Never Gonna Stop
Thunder Kiss 65

The Rolling Stones:
Angie
As Tears Go By
Beast of Burden
Brown Sugar

The Rolling Stones (Cont):
Can't You Hear Me Knocking
Get Off of My Cloud
Gimme Shelter
Happy
Honky Tonk Woman
It's Only Rock and Roll
Jumping Jack Flash
Let's Spend the Night Together
Midnight Rambler
Miss You
Monkey Man
Mothers Little Helper
Play With Fire
Paint it Black
Ruby Tuesday
(I Can't Get No) Satisfaction
She's a Rainbow
Sister Morphine
Start Me Up
Street Fighting Man
Sympathy for the Devil
The Last Time
Time is on My Side
Tumbling Dice
Under My Thumb
You Can't Always Get What You
    Want
Waiting on a Friend
Wild Horses
19th Nervous Breakdown

Romantics:
What I Like About You

Roy Orbison:
Crying
Oh, Pretty Woman
Only the Lonely
Sweet Dreams Baby
You Got It

Rufus Wainwright:
Across the Universe
April Fools
Hallelujah

The Runaways:
Cherry Bomb
Rock N Roll
School Days

Run DMC:
It's Like That
It's Tricky
King of Rock
Walk This Way

Rush:
Anthem
Closer to the Heart
Fly by Night
Limelight
Subdivisions
The Trees
Tom Sawyer
Working Man

Ryan Adams (and the Cardinals):
Hallowennhead
Let It Ride
Oh My Sweet Carolina

25 Great Bass Songs

1. My Generation – The Who
2. Money – Pink Floyd
3. Another One Bites The Dust - Queen
4. Roundabout - Yes
5. Dazed And Confused - Led Zeppelin
6. Badge - Cream
7. Higher Ground - The Red Hot Chili Peppers
8. NIB - Black Sabbath
9. Break On Through - The Doors
10. Taxman - The Beatles
11. Sunshine Of Your Love - Cream
12. London Calling - The Clash
13. Ramble On - Led Zeppelin
14. Boris The Spider - The Who
15. Aqualung - Jethro Tull
16. Come As You Are - Nirvana
17. Stand By Me - Ben E. King
18. Come Together - The Beatles
19. Whipping Post - Allman Brothers Band
20. Brown Eyed Girl - Van Morrison
21. Day Tripper - The Beatles
22. Sweet Emotion - Aerosmith
23. The Joker - Steve Miller Band
24. Longview - Green Day
25. Pump It Up - Elvis Costello

S

Sam Cooke:
Hold On
The Great Pretender
Twistin' the Night Away

Sam and Dave:
Hold On (I'm coming)
Soul Man

Sam the Sham and the Pharaos:
Lil Red Riding Hood
Wooly Bully

Santana:
Black Magic Woman/Gypsy
    Queen
Evil Ways
Soul Sacrifice

Save Ferris:
The World is New

Screamin' Jay Hawkins:
I Put a Spell On You
Whistling Past the Graveyard

Seven Mary Three:
Cumbersome

The Sex Pistols:
Anarchy in the U.K.
God Save the Queen
Holidays in the Sun
Pretty Vacant

Sheryl Crow:
All I Wanna Do
Every Day is a Winding Road
If it Makes You Happy
Leaving Las Vegas
My Favorite Mistake
Soak Up the Sun
Steve McQueen
Strong Enough
The Picture

The Shins:
Sleeping Lessons

Sleater Kinney:
Dig Me Out

Sly and the Family Stone:
Dance to the Music
Everyday People
Family Affair
Hot Fun in the Summertime
I Want To Take You Higher
Music Lover

Silversun Pickups:
Kissing Families
Lazy Eye
Little Lover's so Polite
Panic Switch

Simon & Garfunkel:
Hazy Shade of Winter
Homeward Bound
Mrs. Robinson
Scarborough Fair
Sounds of Silence

Simple Minds:
Don't You (Forget About Me)

Sister Hazel:
All for You

Small Faces:
Itchycoo Park
Tin Soldier
Whatcha Gonna Do About It

Smash Mouth:
All Star
Come On, Come On
I Can't Get Enough of You Baby
Then the Morning Comes
Walkin' on the Sun

The Smashing Pumpkins:
Ava Adore
Bullet With Butterfly Wings
Landslide
Perfect
Rocket
Today
Tonight, Tonight
1979

The Smiths:
How Soon is Now
Panic
Shoplifters of the World Unite
Still Ill

Smokey Robinson (And the Miracles):
I Second That Emotion
Shop Around
Tears of a Clown
The Tracks of My Tears
You Really Got a Hold On Me

Snow Patrol:
Chasing Cars
Shut Your Eyes

Social Distortion:
Bad Luck
Ball and Chain
Born to Lose
Don't Take Me for Granted
Far Behind
Highway 101
I Was Wrong
Prison Bound
Reach for the Sky
Ring of Fire
Story of My Life
When the Angels Sing

Soft Cell:
Tainted Love

Son House:
Death Letter Blues

Sonic Youth:
Dirty Boots
Kool Thing
Sugar Kane
Superstar
Teenage Riot

Soul Asylum:
Black Gold
Run Away Train

Soul Coughing:
Walk Around in Circles

Soundgarden:
Black Hole Sun
Fell On Bad Days
Spoonman

Space Hog:
At Least I Got Laid
In the Meantime
I Want to Live

The Spencer Davis Group:
Gimme Some Lovin'
I'm a Man

Sponge:
Molly (Sixteen Candles)
Plowed

Spooky Tooth:
Evil Woman

Spoon:
Black Like Me
Don't You Evah
I Turn My Camera On
The Way We Get By
Underdog
You Gotta Feel It
You Got Yr. Cherry Bomb

Squeeze:
Tempted

Status Quo:
Bye Bye Johnny
Caroline
Down Down
Pictures of Matchstickmen
Whatever You Want

Stealers Wheel:
Stuck in the Middle With You

Steely Dan:
Do it Again
Reelin in the Years

Steppenwolf:
Born to be Wild
Magic Carpet Ride
The Pusher

Steve Winwood

Steve Winwood is one of the most accomplished musicians of all time. He began as a backup musician for Muddy Waters, John Lee Hooker, Howlin' Wolf, B.B. King, Chuck Berry, Bo Diddley and a number of others when they would tour the United Kingdom. Then when Winwood was just 15 years old, as a member of the Spencer Davis Group, he co-wrote and recorded *Gimme Some Lovin* which would be the bands biggest hit. He later went to co-found the bands Traffic and Blind Faith before embarking on a solo career. To his credit he also played on *Voodoo Chile* with Jimi Hendrix and *With a Little Help from My Friends* with Joe Cocker.

Steve Earle:
Copperhead Road
Galway Girl
Lonelier Than This

Steve Miller:
Fly Like an Eagle
Jet Airliner
Jungle Love
Livin in the USA
Rock'n Me
Take the Money and Run
The Joker
Wild Mountain Honey

Steve Winwood:
Roll With It

Stevie Ray Vaughn:
Crossfire
Life by the Drop
Little Wing
Pride and Joy
Superstition
Texas Flood
Voodoo Child

Stevie Wonder:
Higher Ground
Living for the City
Overjoyed
Signed, Sealed, Delivered
Superstition

Stone Temple Pilots:
Big Empty
Creep
Interstate Love Song
Sex Type Thing

The Stooges:
I Wanna Be Your Dog
Search and Destroy
1969

The Stray Cats:
Rock this Town
Stray Cat Strut

The Strokes:
Hard to Explain
Is This It
Juicebox
Last Nite
Reptilia
Take It or Leave It
The Modern Age
12:51

Styx:
Blue Collar Man
Come Sail Away
Fooling Yourself (The Angry
     Young Man)
Lady
Mr. Roboto
Renegade
The Grand Illusion

Sublime:
Doin' Time
Santeria
What I got
Wrong Way

The Surfaris:
Wipe Out

Sugarcult:
Bouncing Off the Walls

Sugar Hill Gang:
Rappers Delight

Sugar Ray:
Every Morning
Falls Apart
Fly
Someday

Suicidal Tendencies:
Possessed to Skate

Sum 41:
Fat Lip
Still Waiting

Supertramp:
Bloody Well Right
Breakfast in America
Dreamer
Give a Little Bit
Goodbye Stranger

Supertramp (Cont):
Take the Long Way Home
The Logical Song

Susan Tedeschi:
Angel from Montgomery
Talking About

Sweet:
Ballroom Blitz
Fox on the Run

T

Talking Heads:
And She Was
Burning Down the House
Heaven
I Want to Live
Life During Wartime
Psycho Killer
Road to Nowhere
Sugar on My Tongue
Take Me to the River
The Big Country
Wild Wild Life

Tears for Fears:
Everybody Wants to Rule the
    World
Head Over Heels
Shout
Sowing the Seeds of Love

Ted Nugent:
Cat Scratch Fever
Stranglehold

Teenage Fanclub:
Hang On
I Don't Want to Control You
Sparky's Dream
Star Sign
What You Do to Me

Television:
Marquee Moon
See No Evil

The Temptations:
Ain't to Proud to Beg
Get Ready
Just My Imagination
My Girl
Papa was a Rolling Stone
The Way You Do the Things You
    Do

Ten Years After:
I'd Love to Change the World
I'm Going Home
Working on the Road

Them:
Gloria

Theory of a Deadman:
Little Smirk
Hate My Life

Third Eye Blind:
Deep Inside of You
Graduate
How's it Going to Be
Losing a Whole Year
Never let You Go
Non Dairy Creamer
Semi-Charmed Life

Three Dog Night:
Joy to the World
Mama Told Me Not to Come

Tina Turner:
Proud Mary
River Deep Mountain High

The Toadies:
Possum Kingdom
Tyler

Toad the Wet Sprocket:
Something's Always Wrong
Walk on the Ocean

Todd Rundgren:
Bang the Drum All Day

Tom Morello:
Fabled City
The Nightwatchman
Whatever it Takes

Tommy James and the Shondells:
Crimson and Clover

Tommy Tutone:
Jenny/867-5309

Tom Petty (and the Heartbreakers):
American Girl
Breakdown
Don't Come Around Here No More
Don't Do Me Like That
Down South
Free Fallin
I Need to Know
Into the Great Wide Open
I Won't Back Down
Learning to Fly
Listen to Your Heart
Mary Jane's Last Dance
Refugee
Runnin' Down a Dream
Saving Grace
Something in the Air
Square One
The Last DJ
The Waiting
Yer So Bad
You Don't Know How it Feels
You Wreck Me

Tone Loc:
Funky Cold Medina
Wild Thing

Townes van Zandt:
Waitin Around to Die

Traffic:
Dear Mr. Fantasy
Feelin Alright
John Barleycorn Must Die

Traffic (Cont):
Light Up or Leave Me Alone
Rock & Roll Stew
The Low Spark of High Heeled
    Boys

Traveling Wilburys:
End of the Line
Handle Me With Care
Not Alone Anymore
The Devil's Been Busy

Travis:
Closer
Side
Sing
Why Does it Always Rain on Me

T-Rex:
Bang a Gong (Get it on)
Hot Love
Twentieth Century Boy

Tracy Chapman:
Fast Car
Gimme One Reason
Talkin Bout a Revolution

The Troggs:
Wild Thing

Twisted Sister:
I Wanna Rock
We're Not Gonna Take It

U

U-2:
Angel of Harlem
Beautiful Day
Bullet the Blue Sky
Desire
Elevation
Even Better Than the Real Thing
Get on Your Boots
Gloria
In God's Country
I Still Haven't Found What I'm
    Looking For
I Will Follow
Mysterious Ways
New Years Day
One
Pride (In the Name of Love)
Stuck in a Moment
Sunday Bloody Sunday
Sweetest Thing
Vertigo
Walk On
When Love Comes To Town
Where the Streets Have No
    Name
With or Without You

V

Valencia:
Where Did You Go

Vampire Weekend:
A-Punk
M79
Oxford Comma
Teen Jumper

Van Halen:
Can't Stop Loving You
Dance the Night Away
Dancing in the Streets
Eruption
Finish What Ya Started
Hot for Teacher
Jamie's Cryin'
Jump
Panama
Pretty Woman
Right Now
Runnin' With the Devil
Somebody Get Me a Doctor
You Really Got Me
Why Can't This Be Love

Vanilla Fudge:
Shotgun

Van Morrison:
And it Stoned Me
Brand New Day

Van Morrison (Cont):
Brown Eyed Girl
Domino
Into the Mystic
Moondance
Tupelo Honey
Wild Night

The Vapors:
Turning Japanese

Velvet Revolver:
Dirty Pretty Thing
I Fall to Pieces
Slither

Velvet Underground:
I'm Sticking With You
I'm Waiting for the Man
Heroin
Pale Blue Eyes
Sunday Morning
Sweet Jane

The Ventures:
Flight of the Bumblebee
House of the Rising Sun
Sleepwalker
Surf Rider
Walk-Don't Run
Wipe Out

Veruca Salt:
Seether

The Verve:
Bitter Sweet Symphony

The Verve Pipe:
The Freshman
Villains

The Vines:
Get Free
Outta the Way
Ride

The Violent Femmes:
Add It Up
Blister in the Sun
Children of the Revolution
Gone Daddy Gone
Jesus Walking on the Water
Kiss Off

W

The Waitresses:
I Know What Boys Like

The Wallflowers:
One Headlight
Sleepwalker
The Difference
6th Avenue Heartache

War:
Low Rider
Spill the Wine
Why Can't we be Friends

Warren Zevon:
Excitable Boy
Werewolves of London
Prison Grove

Weezer:
Beverly Hills
Buddy Holly
Dope Nose
Don't Let Go
Dreamin'
Everybody Get Dangerous
Hash Pipe
Island in the Sun
Keep Fishin
Knock-Down Drag-Out
Perfect Situation
Photograph

Weezer (Cont):
Pink Triangle
Pork and Beans
Say it Ain't So
The Good Life
Troublemaker
Undone-The Sweater Song

Wheatus:
A Little Respect
In Too Deep
Teenage Dirtbag

The White Stripes:
As Ugly As I Seem
Black Math
Blue Orchid
Bone Broke
Dead Leaves and the Dirty
   Ground
Fell in Love With a Girl
Hello Operator
Hotel Yorba
Hypnotize
Icky Thump
I Just Don't Know What to do
   With Myself
I'm Bound to Pack it Up
In the Cold, Cold Night
Jimmy the Exploder
Little Ghost
Prickly Thorn, But Sweetly Worn
Seven Nation Army
Stop Breaking Down
The Air Near My Fingers
The Hardest Button to Button

The White Stripes (Cont):

The Nurse
There's No Home For You Here
You Don't Know What Love Is
   (You Just do as You're Told)
You're Pretty Good Looking
   (For a Girl)
Your Southern Can is Mine
You've Got Her in Your Pocket
Well It's True That We Love One
   Another
We're Going to be Friends

The Who:

Anyway, Anyhow, Anywhere
Athena
Baba O'Riley
Bargain
Behind Blue Eyes
Christmas
Doctor Jimmy
Getting in Tune
Going Mobile
I Can See for Miles
I Can't Explain
I'm Free
I'm One
Join Together
Let's See Action
Long Live Rock
Love, Reign o'er Me
Magic Bus
My Generation
My Wife
Overture
Pinball Wizard
Pure and Easy

The Who (Cont):

Quadrophenia
Relay
Sally Simpson
See Me, Feel Me
Sensation
Slip Kid
Sparks
Squeeze Box
Substitute
Summertime Blues
The Real Me
The Seeker
You Better You Bet
Welcome
We're Not Gonna Take It
Won't Get Fooled Again
Who Are You
5:15

Wilco:

California Stars
I'm the Man Who Loves You
What Light

Willie Nelson:

Always on My Mind
Blue Eyes Crying In The Rain
Gravedigger
Maria (Shut Up And Kiss Me)
On the Road Again

Wilson Picket:

In the Midnight Hour
Land of 1000 Dances

Wishbone Ash:
Blowin' Free
The King Will Come

Wolf Mother:
Dimensions
Joker and the Thief
Love Train
Vagabond
White Unicorn
Woman

Wrestles Eric:
I Wish it Would Rain
Take the Cash (K.A.S.H)
There Isn't Anything Else
Whole Wide World

Wyclef Jean:
Gone Till November
New Day

12 of the Greatest Bassist of all Time

1. John Entwistle – The Who

2. John Paul Jones – Led Zeppelin

3. Jack Bruce – Cream

4. Flea – Chili Peppers

5. Paul McCartney – The Beatles, Wings, Solo

6. Chris Squire – Yes

7. Geezer Butler – Black Sabbath

8. Geddy Lee – Rush

9. Larry Graham – Sly and the Family Stone

10. Oteil Burbridge (Allman Brothers Band)

11. Roger Waters – Pink Floyd

12. Steve Harris – Iron Maiden

X

XTC:
Dear God
Generals and Majors
Mayor of Simpleton

Y

The Yardbirds:
For Your Love
Got to Hurry
Good Morning Little Schoolgirl
Honey In Your Hips
I'm A Man
I'm Not Talking
I Wish You Would
My Girl Sloopy
Over Under Sideways Down
Smokestack Lightning

Yeah Yeah Yeahs:
Cheated Hearts
Date With the Night
Maps

Yes:
I've Seen All Good People
Owner of a Lonely Heart
Roundabout
Yours Is No Disgrace

Youngbloods:
Get Together

The Young Rascals:
Good Lovin'

The Yardbirds

While the Yardbirds were a part of the British Invasion of the early to mid 1960's they didn't have the same success as other bands of that time in the U.S. However, the Yardbirds do have one distinction that separates them from all other bands of that time or those that came later. They can boast to have at one time featured three separate guitarists that would go on to be considered three of the greatest guitarist of all time. First, there was Eric Clapton who would go on to fame with bands such as *Cream, Blind faith, Derek and the Dominos* along with a stellar solo career.

Second, was Jeff Beck. After he left the Yardbirds, Beck went on to form the *Jeff Beck Group*, and later teamed up with bassist Tim Bogert and drummer Carmine Appice from Vanilla Fudge and released an album as *Beck, Bogert & Appice* before going solo.

Last there was Jimmy Page. When the band broke up Page considered creating a super group with Jeff Beck, Keith Moon and John Entwistle of The Who along with Steve Marriott of the Small Faces and later Humble Pie. Keith Moon joked that the new band "Would go over like a lead balloon" to which John Entwistle added "Like a lead Zeppelin." The super group never materialized and Page tried to put together a new Yardbirds called *The New Yardbirds with Jimmy Page*. The lineup would feature Robert Plant on vocals, his friend John Bonham on drums and session bassist John Paul Jones. Chris Dreja, original member of the Yardbirds, told Page that he couldn't use the Yardbirds name. Remembering the conversation he had with Moon and Entwistle, Page decided to name the new band *Led Zeppelin* and as they say, the rest is history.

Z

The Zombies:
She's Not There
Time of the Seasons

The Zutons:
It's the Little Things We Do
Remember Me
Valerie
Why Won't You Give Me Your
    Love

ZZ Top:
Cheap Sunglasses
Gimme All Your Lovin'
La Grange
Legs
Sharp Dressed Man
Tush

11 Great Music Movies

1. A Hard Days Night

2. This is Spinal Tap

3. Walk the Line

4. Ray

5. La Bamba

6. Great Balls of Fire

7. The Buddy Holly Story

8. Help

9. High Fidelity

10. Anvil

11. School of Rock

Number Bands

L7:
Pretend We're Dead
Shitlist

30 Seconds to Mars:
A Beautiful Lie
From Yesterday
The Kill

.38 Special:
Hold on Loosely

311:
Amber
Down
Love Song

Thank You:

I would like to thank my dad who gave me some suggestions of bands and songs to add and a Very Big Thank You to Jessica Gearhart, who was vital in helping me compile this list. Not only did you give me some very good suggestions to add to my list, which would have otherwise been incomplete, but you helped proofread my work and caught the mistakes that I would have overlooked.